EVERYTHING

A Book of Aphorisms

Aaron Haspel

Second Edition
ISBN: 0-692-58259-2

The author can be reached at ahaspel@gmail.com

The site for the book is everything.aaronhaspel.com

Inquiries about hard copy rights and commercial use should be directed to Lynn Chu at lynn@writersreps.com

To Lisa

CONTENTS

EVERYTHING

INTRODUCTION

This book began with the recognition that I was the sort of writer, or at least wanted to do the sort of writing, best tolerated a sentence or two at a time. Books should rarely be read straight through, and reading this one at a sitting would be like eating the whole pint of ice cream.

The gerundive classification scheme reflects my view that thought must eventually manifest in action to be of any use. I don't mean the vaunted "man of action," who merely executes the instructions of sedentary men, usually long dead, whose very names he often does not know. To provide the instructions is also to act. Aphorisms are often derided as trivial, yet most people rule their lives with four or five of them. The categories spill into each other, as in life.

No book has ever been too short, and this one is no exception. La Rochefoucauld, the greatest of all aphorists, published about six hundred, mostly forgettable. From this collection I would have liked to remove the worst ten, if I could determine which they were. Then I could have removed the next worst ten, and the next, until I had, instead of a book that is too long, no book at all. Among the dross some readers may find a few bits of gold, perhaps for each not the same few bits.

SCHOOLING

Manufacturing stupidity.

Education is free: credentials are expensive.

•

Defang a book by putting it on the syllabus, a painting by putting it in a museum, and a radical by putting him in the ministry.

All intellectuals must begin as pseudo-intellectuals.

•

Of all the lies taught in school, the most vicious is that one ought to perform boring tasks diligently.

•

The least forgiving pedant is the kindergartener in possession of a new fact.

•

It never seems to occur to the teacher who complains of inattentive students that he may not be worth attending to.

Americans take no interest in education but are obsessed with schooling.

•

Nearly every field of human endeavor should be rescued from its admirers.

•

Beware of any discipline that creates its own subject matter.

•

Some subjects are to be studied for their own sake, others for the immunity conferred against their adepts. The vaccination principle applies to education as well as to medicine.

An above-average capacity for boredom is optimal; a superior one is disastrous.

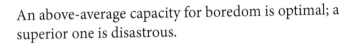

Every business dreams of answering "How much does it cost?" with "How much have you got?" Only college achieves it.

Every business dreams of answering "How much does it cost?" with "How much have you got?" Only college achieves it.

The most effective way to learn is by devoting oneself to a single subject for months at a time. Its opposite is school.

A chief source of the world's ills is that it is run largely by people who did well in school.

A university whose science faculty taught all of its humanities courses would be operative; the reverse would be grotesque.

•

First school spoils us for learning, and then jobs spoil us for work.

•

An education is frequently confused with the flotsam one picks up on the way to acquiring it.

•

Never before have so many spent so much time in school to so little purpose.

READING

The dead alive and busy.
—Vaughan

One reads so as not to believe everything one reads.

●

In hell you are forced to reread continuously all the books you loved when you were twenty.

The self-justifying utterances of murderers, thieves, cowards, blowhards, and madmen all enter the quote books under *Shakespeare*.

•

Many books are least likely to be read by the people who would profit most by reading them.

•

Scholarship

Pompous: Magisterial
Unreliable: Brilliant
Trivial: Valuable
Deranged: Eccentric
Dull: Classic
Duller: Formidable
Stupefying: Encyclopedic

There is little difference between collecting books and collecting porcelain elephants.

•

To read well you have to live a little.

•

We all know intimately many more fictional characters than real ones.

•

Reading old books leavens our fashionable prejudices with a few unfashionable ones.

In fiction murderers and thieves often elicit the reader's sympathy and understanding; snobs and ingrates elicit only his contempt.

•

It takes half a lifetime to learn to read slowly.

•

We say of indelible characters from life that they could be fictional; and from books, that they could be real.

•

The reader properly resents coincidence. Life does not arrange itself to suit him; why should it arrange itself to suit the author?

An unending series of plausible occurrences is impossible in life, and insisted on in fiction.

•

Reading an author's work for his life is like digging up a garden for manure.

•

Cows chew cud, people read newspapers.

•

We weep and blush for fictional characters, never with them.

The reliable narrator is a literary convention.

•

The worst hangover is the morning after you finish a bad book.

•

Read to be contradicted.

•

The great American creeps are Poe and Whitman, and the great American bores are Emerson and Hemingway.

The footnotes are the most important part of corporate annual reports, and the same is often true of non-fiction.

•

Only the very cruelest novelists reproduce dialogue accurately.

•

I have never known anyone book-smart, but book-stupid I see every day.

•

One often hears complaints against morally improving books, as if it were better to be degraded by one's reading.

One does not remember the books so much as become infused with them.

•

Reading, unless it's for writing, is high-class idling.

•

You stir up a lot of sunken knowledge when you reorganize your library.

•

Unbending virtue dies on the page. Bores, prigs, hypocrites, blowhards, martinets — these are the glories of world literature.

Everyone who used to read is now too busy writing.

•

We laugh at novels in which the weather tracks the moods of the characters, yet our own moods mostly track the weather.

•

News is noise.

WRITING

If it had been your exact thought you would have used my exact words.

The ideal work environment for a writer is jail.

•

Prose can hide every vice but vanity.

No book has ever been too short.

•

To be paid for opinions corrupts; and to be paid for particular opinions corrupts absolutely.

•

There are ways of putting things, and each way is a different thing.

•

Surfeit: A group of poets.

To make an epigram, invert a cliché.

•

More is lost in translation from thought to page than from one language to another.

•

Any remark sufficiently clever will eventually be attributed to someone sufficiently famous.

•

It is difficult to write even ten words without wasting one.

Always state the opposing view as persuasively as possible, not to be fair to your opponents but to demoralize them.

•

No style guide can address the chief defect in writing, which is having nothing to say.

•

The reader will often reject, when it is explained and argued for, what he would swallow if it were stated baldly and unadorned.

•

If you write for any other reason than to discover what you think, you are just wasting everybody's time.

Less garbage was written when it had to be written by hand.

•

The ellipsis is the shuffling derelict of punctuation.

•

You may not get the size of audience you deserve, but you always get the kind.

•

Omit, in order of ascending importance, superfluous words, sentences, paragraphs, articles, chapters, and books.

To write is to attempt to assemble a serviceable cottage from the ruins of the castle of thought.

•

Print overawes the illiterate just as machinery overawes the savage.

•

One idea suffices — for a book, for an essay, for an aphorism.

•

Ignorance prevents plagiarism but does not confer originality.

The author who displays his library is like the suspect who leads police to the scene of the crime.

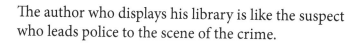

Good critics do not have good taste. They have articulate, consistent taste for which the reader can correct.

Minor masterpiece: What critics call a book they think they might have written themselves with a few more evenings and weekends free.

Read a lot: think some: write a little.

People speak and write in clichés because they see and think in them.

•

By infecting others the writer cures himself.

•

It's easy to be prolific — just keep repeating yourself.

•

Integrity is the writer refusing to make allowances for the reader; philistinism is the reader refusing to make allowances for the writer.

Critics resent artists, but not half as much as artists resent critics.

•

An excellent book could be written consisting entirely of synopses of books that ought to be written.

•

You understand another language not when you can translate it, but when you no longer have to.

•

I ask one thing of literature: that it draw blood.

Read to remember, write to forget.

•

Influence is plagiarism spread thin.

•

Imitation is the most sincere, but parody is the most flattering.

THINKING

*Operations of thought are like cavalry charges in a battle
— they are strictly limited in number, require fresh horses,
and must only be made at decisive moments.*
—Whitehead

The facts never speak for themselves.

•

Every age has its debilitating prejudice; open-mindedness
is ours.

The contrarian attends most scrupulously to conventional wisdom.

•

The tragedy of nonsense is that it banishes difficulty.

•

One can be both right and ridiculous.

•

Certain ideas are so corrosive that they eat through even themselves.

Philosophies, like sweaters, have stray threads, and if you yank on one persistently the whole thing unravels.

•

Polytheism is pre-scientific: monotheism is anti-scientific.

•

The objects of folk-thought change: the patterns never do.

•

If thinkers were not responsible for their disciples they would not take such pains to disavow them.

If you hear hoofbeats, and see stripes, think zebras, not horses.

•

Every logical fallacy is also a valid heuristic.

•

The less a discipline resembles mathematics, the less likely a clever theory is to be true.

•

The serial disciple is often mistaken for an independent thinker.

People say they can't draw when they mean they can't see, and that they can't write when they mean they can't think.

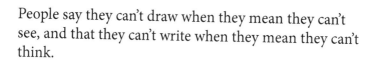

Common sense means you don't know the heuristic.

Profundities are often equivocations — trivially true in one sense, obviously false in another, and deep and subtle only if you do not choose.

First you do not write what you think, then you do not say what you think, and finally you do not think what you think.

The conclusions of philosophy are both true and interesting; but what is true is not interesting, and what is interesting is not true.

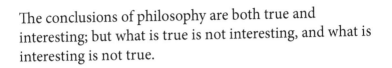

It is not unusual to despise a thinker explicitly and remain completely in his thrall.

•

Nothing so distresses the disciple as the master changing his mind.

•

Stereotypes are folk statistics.

Metaphysics: Logic metastasized.

•

One certainty is often exchanged for another, doubt for certainty occasionally, certainty for doubt almost never.

•

If you wish to make a belief disappear, don't waste your time demonstrating that it is an illusion. Demonstrate that it makes you fat.

•

The critique is usually pertinent, the positive program disastrous.

It is rarer to know when to think than how.

•

What is not indexed may as well not exist.

•

Mental effort dwarfs all other costs.

•

Every effort to know your own mind changes it, sometimes beyond recognition.

Small men flee from a generalization like small animals from a sudden noise — it might not mean danger, but why take a chance?

•

If you must be stupid, at least be lazy.

•

Much wisdom lies on the verge of sense.

•

To change your mind it does not suffice to change your opinion.

The modern mind will countenance any explanation for what you say except that you believe it.

•

What scientists say is not science.

•

Most people, on most matters, are not, in fact, entitled to an opinion.

•

The last heresy is orthodoxy.

To make a reputation as a deep thinker, settle on a single half-truth early, and spend the rest of your life flogging it.

•

Only intellectuals confuse what they know with what they can articulate.

•

The deontologist blindfolds himself, lest his eyes deceive him.

•

They laughed at Edison, they laughed at Fulton, and they laughed at every hopeless crackpot.

The first rule of philosophy is to forget everything you think you know. The second is to forget everything you know.

•

The two great metaphors for society in political philosophy have been machine and organism: thus the two for the individual have been cog and cell.

•

Ingenuity is fatal in philosophers.

•

Thinkers are usually better understood by their detractors than their admirers.

Doubt of the obvious engenders belief in the impossible.

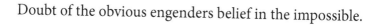

The struggle to assimilate a new idea without disturbing the old ones is hideously physical, like becoming a werewolf.

•

Theory owes far more to practice than practice does to theory.

ERRING

Error is boundless.
Nor hope nor doubt,
Though both be groundless,
Will average out.
—Cunningham

A grudging willingness to admit error does not suffice;
you have to cultivate a taste for it.

•

Where some has failed, more rarely succeeds.

It is so much easier not to be wrong than to be right.

•

Most of what passes for deep thought today can be traced to some misunderstanding of Darwin, Einstein, Heisenberg, or Gödel.

•

To make a grave error clearly and follow it through consistently will place a man among the greatest of philosophers.

•

In the most intractable arguments, one party regards as a question of degree what the other regards as one of kind.

To determine who is expert requires an expert.

•

Untried beliefs are the most firmly held.

•

Most problems are imaginary, and many real problems can be solved by redirecting the attention devoted to the imaginary ones.

•

When someone says that an argument has been discredited he means only that it has gone out of style.

Every contemporary freethinker would believe in Christianity if born in medieval England, and slavery if born in ancient Rome.

•

A new law is passed. We do not read it; would not understand it if we read it; could not foresee its consequences if we understood it; yet hold an unalterable opinion of its merits.

•

The superstitions of a culture are easily discerned: they are the matters on which everyone agrees.

•

Anyone who believes that if you're not part of the solution you're part of the problem is part of the problem.

The inability to fathom a design without a designer leads to hostility to markets in half of the world, and hostility to Darwin in the other half.

•

Our collective delusion that we can fix most problems is another problem we can't fix.

•

Few would deny that the earth was flat if it were a small inconvenience to maintain that it is round.

•

People will cheerfully confess ignorance of a topic and reject indignantly the suggestion that it might debar them from an opinion.

Few experiences are more salutary than losing an argument, but only if you notice.

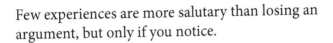

The man who undertakes to rid himself of his illusions and biases can end up like an old painting, improperly cleaned.

•

Philosophy begins by asserting that appearance is not reality — that all is water, or fire, or does not move. It thus begins in sin.

•

The parable of the drunk looking for his keys under the street lamp, where the light is better, explains vast swaths of intellectual history.

Those who believe that what you cannot quantify does not exist also believe that what you can quantify, does.

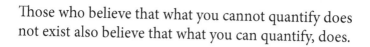

The right side of history — it is a marvel in its way. Five small words, yet is there a contemporary folly it neglects to embrace?

When you have eliminated all other possible explanations, the one that remains, however unlikely, must be that you missed something.

Fools do not suffer fools gladly.

Dark motives lurk where independent beliefs cluster.

•

A man should be pleased to make subtle errors; it means he has avoided the obvious ones.

•

There are entire fields, like psychiatry and philosophy, devoted chiefly to exploding the errors that they create.

•

We pay too little regard to surfaces and too much to depths.

People are confused; it does not follow that the universe is paradoxical.

•

The heretic is not punished for error: he is punished for heresy.

•

Today we believe everything, except what we are told.

•

On many topics it is embarrassing to have an opinion, no matter what it is.

No-brainer, *n.* An idea that is extremely persuasive as long as you don't think about it.

•

To follow your heart is exactly what people who are skilled at manipulating your emotions want you to do.

•

How to Solve Problems

1. Ask if the problem exists.
2. Ask if it is not trivial.
3. Ask if you can do anything about it.
4. Ignore it.

COMPUTING

I did not write a program to generate this book; I am that program.

Everything is analogous to software.

•

How vastly computers will improve our metaphors!

Mathematics: That part of human knowledge in which deduction is reliable.

•

Code is poetry, which says nothing about reading code, but poetry is also code, which says a lot about reading poetry.

•

All computer languages aspire to the condition of LISP.

•

Computers will never be intelligent because humans define intelligence as whatever they do better than computers.

All problems are technical, but not all techniques are adequate.

•

You can't be a polymath without the math.

•

Nobody loves an algorithm.

•

Relativity is uncertainty for infants, Heisenberg for children, and Gödel for adolescents.

Uncertainty for adults is the halting problem.

•

The great divide will be crossed not when a computer can pass a Turing test, but when it can give one.

•

We invent metrics partly to dignify arguments, but mostly to disguise them.

•

Programming is collage at best and pastiche at worst.

Mathematics is not a subject but a method, and ignorance of it is not a gap but a defect.

•

Computers are crude, but so are humans.

•

Efficient search is serendipity's implacable enemy.

•

The more software costs, the worse it is.

Even a computer can do only one thing at a time.

•

People put up with more from software than they ever would from humans.

•

Computers more readily imitate our intelligence than our stupidity.

•

Our ancestors believed in ghosts of people; we believe in multiple regression — ghosts of causes.

The magic of compound interest, natural selection, and many other misunderstood phenomena is the simple algorithm, iterated indefinitely.

LYING

To a quite unwreckable Lie,
To a most impeccable Lie!
To a water-tight, fire-proof, angle-iron, sunk-hinge, time-
lock, steel-faced Lie!
Not a private hansom Lie,
But a pair-and-brougham Lie,
Not a little-place-at-Tooting, but a country-house-with-
shooting
And a ring-fence-deer-park Lie.
—Kipling

The truth is rarely dignified.

The most disinterested truth-seeker still angles for a world of greater rewards for disinterested truth-seekers.

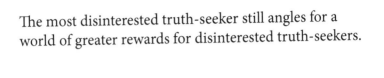

The stupid delude themselves that anything is possible; the clever, that whatever they cannot do cannot be done.

The successful liar is never forgiven for showing us how tawdry the stories are in which we are eager to believe.

The larger truth is always a lie.

We say we feel old when circumstances have momentarily forced us to stop pretending that we are young.

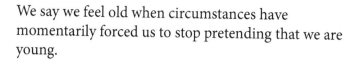

When we can no longer tell ourselves that we are good, we tell ourselves that we are exceptional.

•

Beautiful women become bored with hearing that they are beautiful because it is the only truth they are ever told.

•

If you think about whether you are genuine, too late.

To eliminate uncertainty from data, put it in a chart or graph.

•

To be perfectly sincere one must be very clever or very stupid.

•

We all speak truth to power that we are sure will pay us no mind.

•

A picture lies better than a thousand words.

The expert liar rarely misstates a fact.

•

The more you regard your life as a story the more you edit it.

•

Sometimes one lies to avoid the appearance of lying.

•

To be better it is first necessary to pretend to be; and objections to improvement often masquerade as objections to pretense.

Thoroughgoing rottenness often has nice manners.

•

When we say it's not the money, it's always the money, and when we say it's the money, it's always something else.

•

Optimism is the philosophy of despair.

•

You call a man a cynic when you can't call him wrong, and an idealist when you don't want to.

It is easier to speak the truth than to hear it.

•

Hate speech, *n.* Speech you hate.

•

The fanatic merely acts on his creed. His opposite is the hypocrite, and there is no third alternative.

•

Your terrible secret is that you have no terrible secret.

MATING

Love is an ideal thing, marriage a real thing; a confusion of the real with the ideal never goes unpunished.
—Goethe

Marry for love, divorce for character.

•

Marriages survive not on love but admiration.

If you want to kill your marriage, talk about it.

•

A man will often marry a woman because he is tired of courting her.

•

Trophy wives also have trophy husbands.

•

It matters less if you love your wife than if you like her.

You can divorce your wife but not your generation.

•

Spouses never quite forgive each other their existence before they met.

•

Marry a beautiful woman to be envied, an intelligent woman to be fascinated, and a thrifty woman to be happy.

•

If the object of desire is rich, we call it gold-digging; if handsome, lust; if clever, fascination; and if he has no discernible appeal, we call it love.

The honeymoon ends with the first sigh.

•

The more logical feminists, beginning by giving up sex roles, end by giving up sex.

•

Confusion about pronouns and antecedents will be feminism's enduring legacy.

•

Once you see human interaction as a contest to signal mating fitness, you never see it as anything else.

When a man publicly declares that he loves his wife he means he doesn't like her.

•

Eye candy is rarely ear candy.

•

Countless "dysfunctional" marriages persist in spite of the therapist's disapproval. The better term would be "functional."

•

Between machismo and boyishness lies a large and almost entirely unexploited market niche.

Only women who dress well undress well.

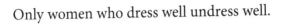

If choice trumped biology, men would divorce their children instead of their wives.

If choice trumped biology, men would divorce their children instead of their wives.

Women lead, pretending to follow; men follow, pretending to lead.

No universally acclaimed institution has a more dismal track record than marrying for love.

WORKING

Business is more agreeable than pleasure; it interests the whole mind more continuously, and more deeply.
—Bagehot

Jobs are like jail, except with time added for good behavior.

•

Restaurants fail more frequently than gas stations because no one dreams of quitting his corporate job to open a gas station.

Expertise makes one peremptory, but peremptoriness does not make one expert.

•

Passion: An overwhelming urge to spend your life at something you don't do especially well.

•

The business of America is busyness.

•

Our doctors have cured so much, so little of it disease.

The impeccably credentialed are always loyal to the reigning order.

•

Blaming an actor for being a narcissist is like blaming a tiger for being a carnivore.

•

To manage people effectively you must not only accept but praise work that you could have done better yourself.

•

You haven't learned a trade until you are surprised to see it done well.

In tedium lies opportunity.

•

It is when we recognize our hopeless inadequacy at everything else that we discover our vocation.

•

An actor can be ugly and still have no talent.

•

The most interesting things to do are the dullest to watch.

Professional courtesy is a conspiracy against the public.

•

The product of too great a contempt for bad work is no work.

•

Executives rail against government bureaucracy from the confines of a corporate bureaucracy that would shame an apparatchik.

•

Every nuisance that you could fix but tolerate instead represents a small, private, but unmistakable regression to savagery.

A relentlessly cheerful, upbeat, can-do attitude is a highly effective form of bullying.

•

Design is the residue of luck.

•

Failure is always an option. Often it is the best option.

•

The good customer never reminds the shopkeeper how good a customer he is.

More successful enterprises have been created for spite than for money.

•

A career is tolerable only in retrospect.

•

Rather than spend time at work, spend the time you do spend at work working.

•

Working on an easy task when you are capable of a hard one is a particularly insidious form of procrastination.

When you don't need a doctor, you really don't need one.

•

The more you know how things work, the less you expect them to.

•

The Third Culture is Engineering.

•

Science progresses by funeral, engineering by disaster.

The psychological travails of Western man stem mostly from the fact that he can be idle and not starve.

•

The glass ceiling may be *trompe l'oeil*.

•

If you aren't supposed to use people, what do you do with them?

•

Ask if you do your job well, but first ask if it ought to be done at all.

Humanity for the first time is burdened with a vast proletariat of literate, ambitious, and demanding people who can't really do anything.

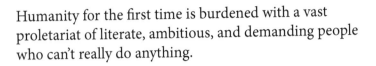

Intellectuals are hostile to businessmen chiefly because the public prefers what the businessmen are selling.

•

Whatever the world's greatest criminal mastermind is doing, it's sure to be legal.

•

Indolence wears many subtle disguises; sometimes it appears as fastidious disgust for the second-rate.

When did "personality" become a job description?

•

Effort is like medicine: half of it is useless or harmful, and the trick is to know which half.

GETTING

You never find people endeavoring to convince you that you may live very happily upon a plentiful fortune.
—Johnson

Money doesn't solve problems, it dissolves them.

•

You can have anything you want, provided it's the only thing you want, and it's not worth having.

Success: A not entirely unbroken record of failure.

•

The dirtiest money can be laundered in two generations.

•

It speaks well for money that people feel compelled to say it can't buy everything.

•

It's all fun and games until somebody gets paid.

It hurts less to give up the luxury than the idea that you can afford it.

•

The more you have, the more you need.

•

Get-rich-quick schemes do less harm than get-wise-quick ones.

•

No one is unprincipled until he is successful.

To reduce the value of anything one need only try to sell it.

•

For favors you pay three times over.

•

People will pay dearly for the right to bore you.

•

A thing got rid of is a joy forever.

The American upper middle class has largely given up sex and alcohol in favor of litigation and insurance fraud.

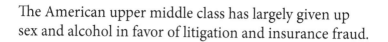

Wealth can be pursued cooperatively, but fame is to the death.

It is best that something as permanent as envy be directed at something as transient as money.

The very rich and the very poor both spend most of their time thinking about money.

Commercial success frees you to pursue further commercial success.

•

Some men, like Balzac's Goriot, are made of money, and when it ends so do they.

•

To gauge opinion, check bond prices.

•

So many who refuse to sell out, so few with anything worth buying.

The joy of money lies less in what one does than in what one might do.

•

A man will reveal the most intimate details of his sex life before he will show you his tax return.

•

Inequalities of wealth and power pale beside inequality of merit.

•

Halving your actual possessions doubles your effective ones.

The only known cure for materialism is poverty.

•

No one can be bought, but everyone can be rented.

RULING

In '37 Stalin made a hash
Of party loyalists and army brass.
Decimation: One in ten are shot.
What's the word when one in ten are not?

A regime of many laws is a great aid in the destruction of men of large virtues and petty faults.

•

No government strong enough to provide liberty is weak enough to preserve it.

Hard cases make bad law, and good law makes hard cases.

•

The worse the government, the longer the speeches.

•

Abroad we make our soldiers pretend to be policemen, and at home we let our policemen pretend to be soldiers.

•

No government suppresses thought and speech as effectively as your friends and neighbors do.

Tardiness is the rudeness of kings, and punctuality the necessary politeness of their subjects.

•

Every genocide is an accidental eugenics program.

•

Ideologies must be classed not by what they intend to build but by what they intend to destroy.

•

If truth were ever spoken to it power would be grateful.

Policy begets policy.

•

A well-conducted police state pardons a few prisoners now and then; this persuades the populace that the rest are guilty.

•

A government not of men but of laws — written by men, interpreted by men, and enforced by men.

•

There are always and everywhere two political parties: the Ins and the Outs. The rest is advertising.

Inflict the punishment, and the crime will be inferred.

•

The favorite tool of the politician is the organization that professes itself above politics.

•

Countries are artificial: cities are natural.

•

One ought to be a bit embarrassed to win an election.

Men form alliances first not to be stolen from, and then to steal.

•

A police state always employs the children to cow the adults.

•

Many privileges are granted on the implied condition that they will not be exercised.

•

People would rather be ruled by their own kind than well.

Politicians do not place their personal interests before the national interest: they regard them as indispensable to the national interest.

•

All arguments over process are in fact over policy.

•

People will stand for hardship from their rulers but not for insult.

•

The incorruptible politician merely prefers power to money.

Parents, and governments, pursue order, not justice.

•

Leader: A megalomaniac whose luck has not yet run out.

•

Every new power allies itself with the dispossessed, for the possessed are its competition.

•

No one wants equality except with his betters.

Punishment deters best when regarded as expiation.

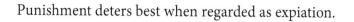

The practicing capitalist is a capitalist; the practicing anarchist is a terrorist; the practicing socialist is a thief.

The conservative rarely vouches for the health of the patient; he merely prefers the disease to the cure.

By the time a suit reaches the Supreme Court any party that can be ruined has been.

Vox populi, vox bubuli.

•

Revolutions spare nothing but the machinery of the state at which they are ostensibly directed.

•

Revolution gets awfully good press, considering its track record.

•

The less you are contradicted, the stupider you become. The more powerful you become, the less you are contradicted.

That no one is above the Law is less a principle than a threat.

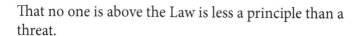

Men can always be found to do the king's bidding without asking so much as the king's shilling in return.

Ｔhe people are flattered more obsequiously than the monarch ever was.

Those who attack the status quo on the grounds that nothing could be worse are usually proposing something worse.

The Gods of Liberty, Equality, Justice, and The People have demanded more human sacrifice than all other divinities combined.

•

Anything can be conjured into existence by empowering a committee to suppress it.

•

That anyone would wish for power is sufficient reason to deny it to him.

•

Nobody says "it's the law" about a good law.

The revolutionary treats the oppressed as the defense lawyer treats the client: under no circumstances are they to speak for themselves.

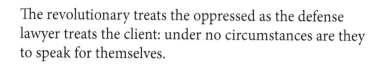

Taxes, regarded as the price of indifference, are a bargain.

The tyrant concerned for his reputation must concentrate his fire on the inarticulate, who don't leave pesky memoirs behind. Kill peasants, not Jews.

There can be no tyranny without opacity.

The revolutionary is nine parts hatred and envy of the oppressor, and one part sympathy and love for the oppressed.

·

Every party looks its best out of power.

·

Man is everywhere in chains, which imposes a substantial evidentiary burden on those who claim that he is born to be free.

·

I don't want to be a subject of my government. I don't even want to be a shareholder. I just want to be a customer.

Revolution is seeded by abuse and watered by reform.

•

Liberty, Equality, or Fraternity.

•

The people never means quite all of them.

SELF-LOVING

We all come into this world with our little egos equipped with individual horns. If we don't blow them, who will?
—DeWitt

We are what we fear to appear to be.

•

We talk not to say something, but to show something.

Demanding respect is the infallible sign of not deserving it.

•

History is the events leading up to my life; biography is the events leading up to my death.

•

We are just deep enough to wish for depths.

•

It is a peculiar hell, this world in which everyone is always ready for his close-up.

Those who profess indifference to the opinions of others might advertise it less.

•

Mute inglorious Miltons, flowers born to blush unseen and waste their sweetness on the desert air, are extinct, and I miss them.

•

Being bad at math does not make you good at art.

•

We laugh mostly to show that we understand the joke.

An American has no betters, as far as he knows.

•

We are such accomplished liars because we get so much practice on ourselves.

•

To regard oneself as the exception is the rule.

•

Knowing the answer does not oblige you to raise your hand.

Salieri was a lot better at music than you are at anything.

•

You can ignore the opinions of others if you know your own worth, and a persistent delusion works equally well.

•

We praise in others what we wish to have noticed in ourselves.

•

It is our former selves that we especially loathe.

I owe my sublime indifference to awards, prizes, and all forms of official recognition to never receiving any.

•

An idiot especially resents being treated like an idiot.

•

The polite conversationalist, when interrupted by a monologue, smiles, and waits his turn, before resuming his own.

•

Everyone is vain about his choice of what not to be vain about.

The most grievous insult is the affected modesty of the truly accomplished.

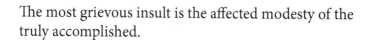

The Dunning-Kruger effect is especially pronounced in people who know what the Dunning-Kruger effect is.

We reserve our warmest admiration, not for what is utterly beyond us, but for what we secretly believe we might have done ourselves on our very best day.

We all have the strength to refuse what we have not been offered.

Greed often sharpens the mind; vanity never.

•

We are all such good people, and we all do such horrid things.

•

Nothing reduces status like being caught grubbing for it.

•

If it has never crossed your mind that you might be stupid, you are.

It is impossible to recognize your betters until you acknowledge that they exist.

BEING

Identity, that spectator of what he calls himself,
That net and aggregate of energies in transient
combination.
—Cunningham

All appears as it would if it were what it is.

•

One is human insofar as one is difficult to model.

Life has heuristics: only games have rules.

•

No one thinks to correct hypocrisy by aligning his beliefs with his actions.

•

One of truth's greatest enemies is collegiality.

•

Fortune does not favor the bold; it only encounters them more often.

Elision is the mother of decision.

•

Certain qualities — skepticism, iconoclasm, willpower —
are fixed in quantity, and must be apportioned wisely.

•

A reputation for virtue is its own reward.

•

Law of Moral Parsimony: The most probable explanation
is the least flattering.

Inopportunity is always knocking.

•

Men will never be as good at being men as cats are at being cats.

•

The future will marvel that we regarded "be yourself" as sound moral advice.

•

Never attribute to malice what can be explained by stupidity, or to stupidity what can be explained by drug abuse.

You never violate your principles: you only discover that they are not what you thought they were.

•

Nice isn't funny, funny isn't nice, and nice isn't even especially nice most of the time.

•

Too bourgeois is an irritant, not bourgeois enough a disaster.

•

The dream of escaping oneself can be realized, in part, by escaping other people's ideas of oneself.

A man can adapt to nearly anything, but only two or three times.

•

Wanna Bet and Sticks and Stones — the modern adult would do well to recover these timeless principles of the playground.

•

Better deceived than distrustful.

•

As sympathy broadens, it also shallows.

There's not much point in age without wisdom, or youth without folly.

•

Whatever you have done, you are the sort of person who would do that.

•

Through the veil of routine you sometimes glimpse what you are really doing.

•

Whoever despises the means does not desire the end.

Habits acquired in jest are retained in sorrow.

•

You attenuate your strengths by too assiduously correcting your defects.

•

People with little that they want to do find a lot that they have to do.

•

The first trick every utterly unreasonable person masters is a calm and reasonable appearance.

The fat man should never eat the last doughnut.

•

Manners are the cargo cults of morals.

•

The lives of desperation that most men lead at least used to be quiet.

•

The value of privacy can be judged by everyone's rush to dispose of what little he has left.

Moral progress is only economic progress: men in the mass have the ethics they can afford.

•

"If it ain't broke, don't fix it" would be a more telling argument if everything were not, in fact, broke.

•

Tact is the art of being rude.

•

No one hates or envies insincerely.

Nothing tastes quite like the hand that feeds you.

•

All special snowflakes look exactly alike without a microscope.

•

People will like you if you like them, which is too high a price.

•

Anger impairs judgment but improves memory.

What can be done can usually be undone, but at considerable expense.

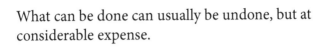

We wish, not to be understood, but to be misunderstood exactly as we misunderstand ourselves.

•

Adaptive is not optimal.

•

Boredom is often fatal, though it never appears on the coroner's report.

The petty soul favors the grand gesture.

•

The end does not justify the means; it is the means.

•

We all want to be happy, just not at the expense of the qualities that makes us unhappy.

•

What you lose with age is not so much capacities as the illusion that you ever had them.

Whatever one does well one is sure to do too often.

•

Attention begets all virtue, distraction all vice.

•

What we call maturity is mostly fatigue.

•

Most evil is done routinely.

And now abideth sloth, greed, fear, these three; but the greatest of these is sloth.

•

There is always a ceiling, and never a floor.

•

The one simple thing that will change your life is to stop believing that one simple thing will change your life.

•

Wisdom is the great consolation prize.

SEEMING

Religion, art, taste, and other delusions.

We are constrained not by the tiny number of possibilities that we reject, but by the vast number that never occur to us.

•

If you wish to change a man's beliefs, you have to give him something to replace them.

Nobody knows what he's missing.

•

Sometimes it is the work of art that looks at you and finds you wanting.

•

An outré appearance generally hides a conventional mind.

•

The artist-provocateur does more damage than he knows: he immunizes his audience against shock, and who cannot be shocked cannot be moved.

Bad art leads to bad restaurant service.

•

Civilization is artifice: to be natural within it is a supreme affectation.

•

Alienation is maladaptation.

•

Without the label you can't tell the difference.

What passes for sanity is only people's fortunate refusal to take their own ideas seriously.

•

Shortly before death comes nostalgia.

•

Data and science have become our garlic and wolfsbane.

•

It is one's worst taste that is most characteristic.

The snob is a penitent, who flogs himself for what he likes with what he thinks he ought to.

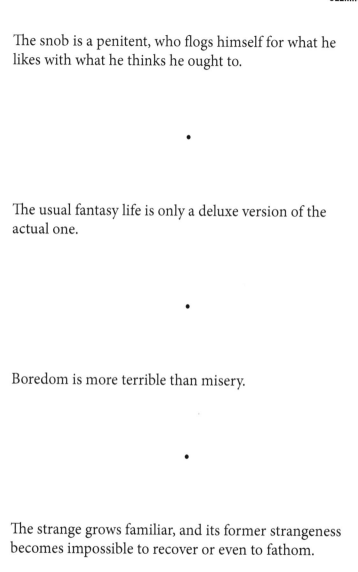

The usual fantasy life is only a deluxe version of the actual one.

Boredom is more terrible than misery.

The strange grows familiar, and its former strangeness becomes impossible to recover or even to fathom.

People praise sincerity in art because they cannot bear the idea that an artist can imitate their deepest thoughts and feelings while remaining unmoved by them.

•

Where there are no constraints there can be no art.

•

Sanity is correspondence at the expense of coherence. Madness is coherence at the expense of correspondence.

•

In the movies you can smoke all you like, but you can't cough without dying.

Man oscillates continuously between wishing to remain exactly as he is and wishing to become something, anything else.

•

Inner peace, simplicity, and harmony with the universe come to us all — very soon now, no hurry.

•

Religion will persist forever because of reality's stubborn refusal to accord with our primitive notions of justice.

•

As I interpret Genesis, the original sin is ennui.

Beauty that does not in some way modify your standards for beauty is kitsch.

•

Religion without doctrine or ritual is nothing, or as we now say, spirituality.

•

Whatever you think you like — are you sure you like it? Or do you like being the sort of person who likes it?

•

At bad art you cry: at great art you cringe.

Good art does not ennoble, it merely refines; and bad art does not degrade, it merely coarsens.

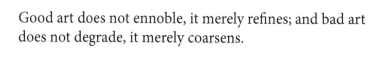

Guilty pleasure: What you are afraid your inferiors might like.

The chief puzzle in aesthetics is not disagreement, but agreement. To a first approximation, everyone likes the same things.

Where once you had to confess your sins to be saved, it now suffices to confess your disease.

Art corrupts politics more than politics corrupts art.

•

God would satisfy no one without His viciousness and caprice.

•

In a friend it is easier to tolerate bad character than bad taste.

•

Primitives and children often have crude taste, but only civilized adults have bad taste.

Taste is quality divided by expense.

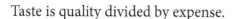

Any sufficiently naïve use of the word "science" is indistinguishable from the word "magic."

Any sufficiently naïve use of the word "science" is indistinguishable from the word "magic."

The audience will always be out of step with the artist, for one is just arriving at what the other has long since put out of mind.

The hard sciences killed God, natural selection buried Him, variance drove a silver stake through His heart, and yet He will not die.

Our awareness of what we deserve, but lack, is surpassed only by our blindness to what we have, but do not deserve.

•

Whether joy and suffering are regarded as immoral depends on which comes first.

•

Exceptionally bad art sometimes acquires a constituency, as famous murderers attract marriage proposals.

•

Western religious and secular thought have finally converged on the idea that to be good it is necessary only to believe that you are.

Belief in karma is the coward's revenge.

•

Most of the great art ever produced has been destroyed, forgotten, or unrecognized.

REMEMBERING

The obscurest epoch is today.
—Stevenson

We remember what we believe, and believe what we remember.

•

We call past ages unhappy with no better warrant than that we suppose we would have been unhappy in them.

Civilization has always existed only in enclaves, and whoever would universalize it is its unwitting enemy.

•

The past, like a mirror, is best gazed into from a middle distance; you can see nothing close up or far away.

•

The historical imagination is the recognition that then was someone else's now.

•

Each photograph in the album is a tiny buttress of age with youth, of a ruined present with a glorious past.

Chivalry is moribund, but every war kindles a recrudescence.

•

History is apocryphal.

•

Into every 1789 a little 1793 must fall.

•

People throughout history have died mostly of being in the way.

The belief that one is entirely self-created has been possible in only a few times and places. It is an accident of circumstance.

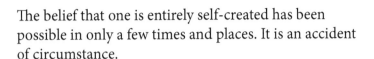

Most of the people who have ever lived have been almost entirely inarticulate, and we know nothing about them.

•

All people at all times have annals; but only some at a few times have history.

•

History is not progress; yet without the idea of progress there can be no history.

That no change is possible was the ancient superstition; that any change is possible is the modern one.

•

Etiquette and ritual are punctiliously observed long after traditions and religions have died, as fingernails still grow on a corpse.

•

We are more like our contemporaries than we imagine, and less like our ancestors.

•

Chronology is to history what arithmetic is to mathematics.

The archetype of the modern intellectual is not the dry specialist, as the nineteenth century foresaw, but the interdisciplinary huckster.

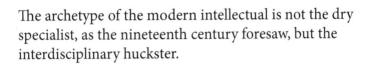

Today's *reductio*, tomorrow's reality.

Eventually one wearies of strangling the last king with the guts of the last priest.

Yesterday the great enemy of democracy was distinction of birth; today it is distinction of wealth; tomorrow it will be distinction.

Many historical figures supposed to be influential are chiefly so among the cataloguers of influence.

•

History is made forwards and written backwards, which is the chief source of error in both the making and the writing.

•

Civilization expire, unnoticed, in a rabble of compilers, curators, connoisseurs, encyclopedists, mashers-up, aficionados.

•

"It was a culture," the historian will write a century from now, "that found it necessary to invent the word *unironically*."

More people fear the past than the future.

•

Those who can remember the past are condemned to tell those who cannot what part of it we are now repeating.

•

Humanity has progressed vastly with how, less with what, and not at all with why.

•

Our descendants will regard us for hanging men as we regard our ancestors for hanging dogs.

The great lesson of history is that it exists.

•

Today we hear silence as our ancestors heard music.

NOTHING

You cannot have a contemporary prison without contemporary furniture.
—Clouseau

The modern world does not create our ills; it only drags them into the light.

•

Tell me what you hate, and I will tell you how old you are.

Imagination is anthropomorphism run amok.

•

Personality varies like men's fashion — a quarter-inch of width in the tie or length in the cuff.

•

To get on with children, treat them like adults; to get on with adults, treat them like children.

•

A country becomes civilized when its inhabitants can form an orderly queue.

One is asked to be reasonable and expected to be moderate.

•

The great contemporary leveler of class distinctions is automated spell-checking.

•

Diseases have fashions, but hypochondria is always in style.

•

We know how to lose at Natural Selection, but how do you win?

Behind the insult "calculating" a whole moral history of humanity lies hidden.

•

A civilization with elaborate manners is already half-dead.

•

The chief perquisite of belonging to a race or creed is a lifetime pass to tell nasty jokes at its expense.

•

It's easy to get away with murder, except the one you want to commit.

The best possible recommendation is from someone who hates it for a reason that would make you like it.

•

We all suffer from a variety of psychiatric disorders, which used to be known as personality.

•

Great geniuses possess no extraordinary qualities, only ordinary qualities in exceptional measure.

•

Shame seems to have peaked as a verb just when it has disappeared as a noun.

Therapy encourages the patient to think and talk about himself — which is what induced him to seek therapy.

•

In a democratic age manners and mores spread from top to bottom, then from bottom back to top.

•

The height of a civilization can be judged by its mathematics and its music.

•

Faces, like cases, collapse under scrutiny.

The likeable never know whether they are liked for themselves or for their likeability.

•

Whatever is unnecessary is pernicious.

•

There is a level of fame where it is no longer necessary to be interesting, and a higher level where it is no longer possible.

•

The provocateur is the most fortunate of men: he receives all credit for his wisdom and no blame for his folly.

Many people kill themselves because they are tired of repeating themselves.

•

Candor is honesty's poor relation.

•

Evil, to a first approximation, is stupidity.

•

Now that the symptoms of genius have been thoroughly advertised, one sees a great deal more of the symptoms.

Youth buys Age, and Age buys Youth.

•

For purposes of conversation the world can be divided into two classes: too young to talk, and too old to listen.

•

Youth is lost like money — gradually, then suddenly.

•

Nothing is more vulgar than a horror of vulgarity.

The Jewish kid who spray-paints a swastika on the synagogue to make the local TV news — this is the guiding metaphor for our time.

•

An electronic device that tracked your location at all times used to be a condition of parole.

•

Behavioral is to classical economics as relativistic is to classical mechanics.

•

When God wants to test you, He sends a person of good character who shares none of your opinions.

When God wants to punish you, He sends a person of bad character who shares all of your opinions.

No party is boring when regarded as field work in cultural anthropology.

•

People who do not say what they mean usually do not know what they mean.

•

Talk comes in two sizes — big and small.

•

To hate something properly you must have liked it once.

No cynic would argue for cynicism.

•

Now that all have prizes, has everybody won?

•

We cry wolf and then the world ends.

ACKNOWLEDGEMENTS

The people who induced me, in various ways, to inflict these on the world in this form include Colby Cosh, Laura Demanski, Jim Guida, Adam Gurri, John Faithful Hamer, Barbara Haspel, Charles Haspel, Tamar Haspel, Julius Lemos, Colin Marshall, Nassim Nicholas Taleb, Terry Teachout, James Valliant, and Eric Weinstein. All complaints should be directed to them. Greg Linster read an early draft and provided valuable comments. Danielle Faribault designed the interior. My wife Lisa designed the cover.

31813754R00105

Made in the USA
Middletown, DE
13 May 2016